# How People Get Married

by Caroline Arnold

Illustrated by Jane Kendall

Franklin Watts
New York   London   Toronto   Sydney
1987

Library of Congress Cataloging-in-Publication Data

Arnold, Caroline.
  How people get married.

  (Ceremonies and celebrations)
  Includes index.
  Summary: Briefly discusses marriage customs in
the United States before, during, and after the
wedding.
    1. Weddings—United States—Juvenile literature.
2. Marriage service—United States—Juvenile
literature.
3. Marriage customs and rites—United States—
Juvenile literature. [1. Weddings. 2. Marriage customs
and rites]
I. Kendall, Jane F., ill. II. Title. III. Series.
HQ745.A76   1987        392'.5'0973        86-13126
ISBN 0-531-10096-0

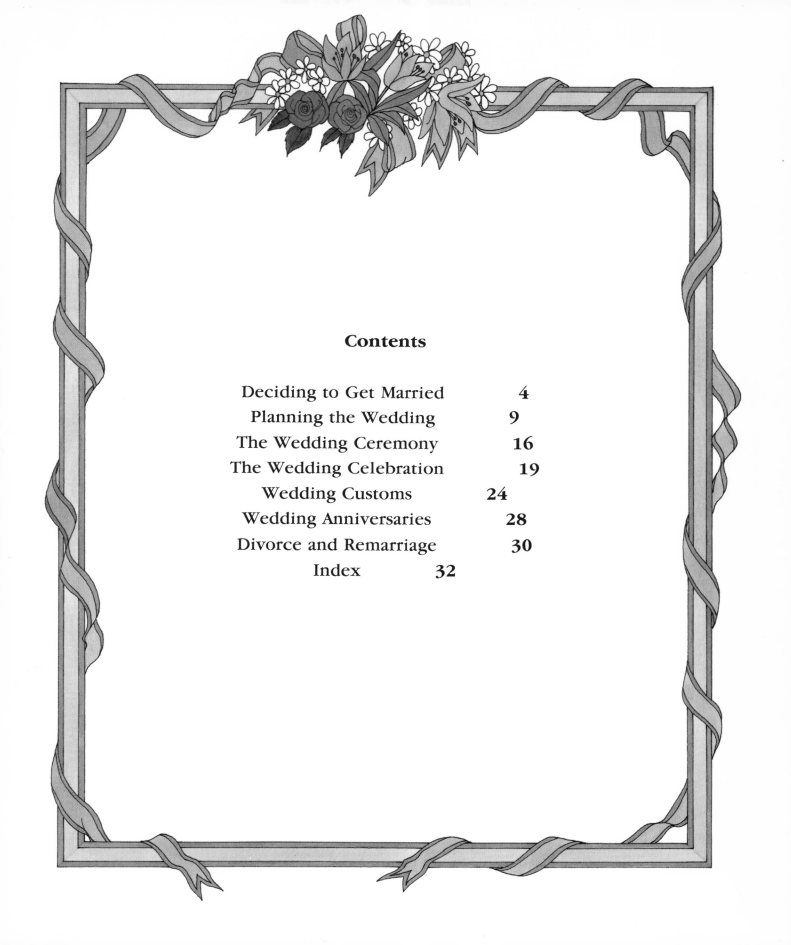

# Contents

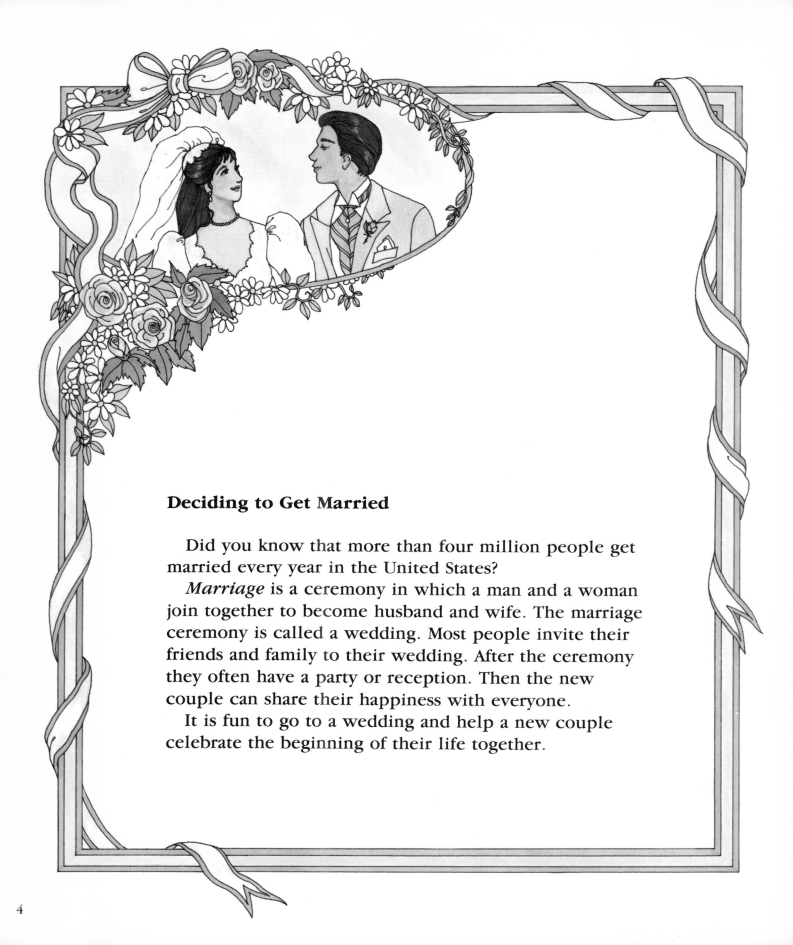

## Deciding to Get Married

Did you know that more than four million people get married every year in the United States?

*Marriage* is a ceremony in which a man and a woman join together to become husband and wife. The marriage ceremony is called a wedding. Most people invite their friends and family to their wedding. After the ceremony they often have a party or reception. Then the new couple can share their happiness with everyone.

It is fun to go to a wedding and help a new couple celebrate the beginning of their life together.

Usually when a man and a woman decide to marry they first become *engaged*. Often the man gives the woman an *engagement ring*. Usually the ring has a diamond or other valuable stone in it. The woman wears the ring on the fourth finger of her left hand.

When two people become engaged they may celebrate by having an engagement party. They may also announce their engagement in the newspaper. The announcement usually tells where the man and woman live, who their parents are, and where they work or go to school. You can look in your newspaper to find out who is planning to be married in your community.

When a man becomes engaged he is called a *fiancé* by his future wife. She is called a *fiancée* by him.

It used to be a custom that a man had to ask a woman's father for permission to marry her. If the father refused then they could not marry. Today most couples discuss their marriage plans with their families. However, they do not need permission unless they are too young to get a marriage license.

A marriage is a legal union between two people. Whenever two people get married they must get a *marriage license*. Every state has its own rules about what you need to do to get a marriage license.

In most states you must be eighteen years or older to marry without your parents' permission. Even with your parents' consent, you must be over sixteen to marry in most states. Most states also require that a man and a woman have blood tests before getting married. These tests help to make sure that their children will be healthy.

### Planning the Wedding

Once a couple has decided to get married, they must choose where, when, and how to do it.

People have weddings in all kinds of places. Most people have weddings in churches or synagogues. However, many people have weddings at home, in gardens, or at hotels.

People can be married in either a *religious ceremony* or a *civil ceremony*. A religious ceremony is performed by a minister, priest, or rabbi. A civil ceremony is performed by a public official such as a judge or a justice of the peace. On board a ship, the captain can perform a wedding ceremony.

A couple planning a wedding may want other people to be part of the ceremony. These people are the *wedding attendants*.

The bride may choose a few close friends to be her attendants. They are called *bridesmaids*. One of them is the *maid of honor*. The groom may choose *groomsmen* as his attendants. Some of them may act as ushers at the wedding ceremony. One will be his *best man*.

The maid of honor and best man stand next to the bride and groom during the wedding ceremony. They help them if they are needed.

Sometimes a bride and groom choose a child to be an attendant too. A young girl can be a *junior bridesmaid* or a *flower girl*. A boy can be a *ring bearer*. The ring bearer carries the wedding ring on a small pillow. Usually the ring is pinned to the pillow so it cannot fall off and get lost. If there is no ring bearer, the best man usually holds the ring for the groom. The maid of honor holds the ring for the bride.

Some weddings are simple. Others are very fancy. However, in almost all weddings the bride and groom wear special clothes.

The groom may wear a suit. Or he may wear more formal clothes such as a tuxedo. Since most people do not own formal clothes, they often rent them for a wedding.

Whenever we think of a bride, we think of a woman in a beautiful long white dress. Most brides do wear white dresses but not always. White is often used at weddings because it is a symbol of purity. A bride's dress sometimes has a *train*. A train is a long part of the skirt of the dress which trails on the floor behind the bride.

In most religious ceremonies it is a custom for a bride to wear a veil. In some ceremonies the veil is so thick the bride must be led down the aisle. Usually the veil is worn over the face for the first part of the wedding ceremony. After the ceremony is over, the bride lifts the veil and the groom kisses her.

Usually the bride chooses dresses for her attendants in a style that will go with her own dress. The bride also chooses the flowers she and her attendants will carry. The flowers may be bought or picked from a garden.

After the date and place for the wedding have been decided, the bride and groom must choose whom to invite. Because a wedding is a formal occasion, the invitation is often formal. It may be handwritten or printed.

When you are invited to a wedding, you should give a gift to the bride and groom. Wedding gifts are usually meant to help the bride and groom furnish their new home. After the wedding, the bride and groom will send thank you notes for all their gifts.

Sometimes friends of the bride and groom give a party for them before the wedding. The party is called a *wedding shower*. Shower gifts also help to furnish the new home. A kind of wedding party given by pioneer women for a new bride was called a *pounding*. Each woman brought a pound of food such as flour, butter, or sugar. These foods helped the new bride supply her kitchen.

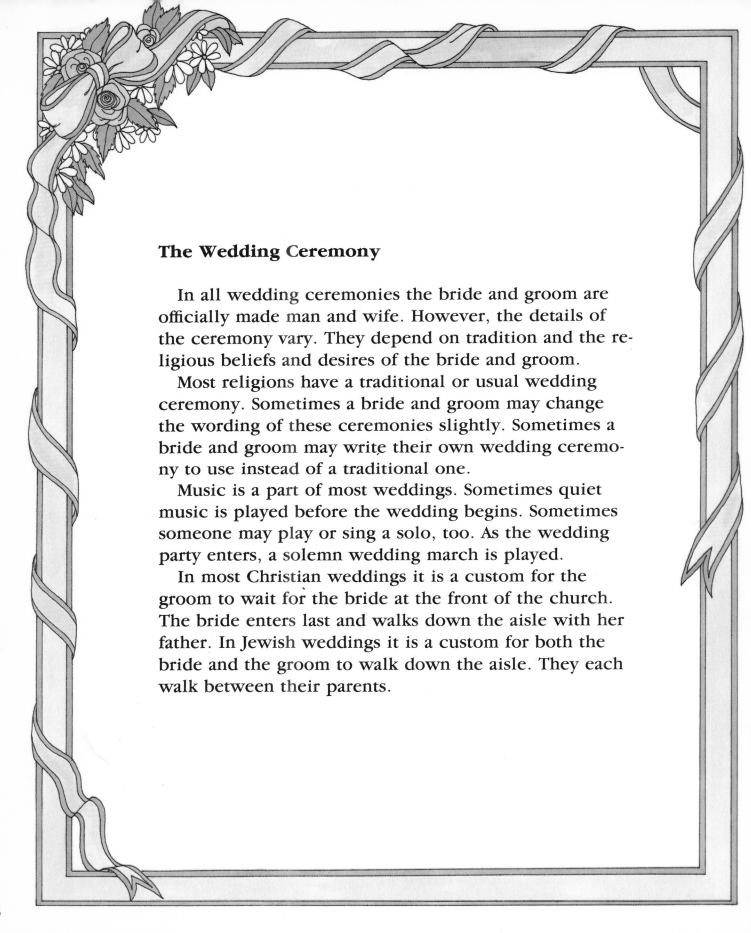

## The Wedding Ceremony

In all wedding ceremonies the bride and groom are officially made man and wife. However, the details of the ceremony vary. They depend on tradition and the religious beliefs and desires of the bride and groom.

Most religions have a traditional or usual wedding ceremony. Sometimes a bride and groom may change the wording of these ceremonies slightly. Sometimes a bride and groom may write their own wedding ceremony to use instead of a traditional one.

Music is a part of most weddings. Sometimes quiet music is played before the wedding begins. Sometimes someone may play or sing a solo, too. As the wedding party enters, a solemn wedding march is played.

In most Christian weddings it is a custom for the groom to wait for the bride at the front of the church. The bride enters last and walks down the aisle with her father. In Jewish weddings it is a custom for both the bride and the groom to walk down the aisle. They each walk between their parents.

In many wedding ceremonies the bride and groom give each other rings. Sometimes only the groom gives the bride a ring. The ring is a sign of their everlasting love. It is worn on the fourth finger of the left hand. If the bride has an engagement ring she takes it off so that the wedding ring can go on first. It is a tradition that a man and a woman never take off their wedding rings as long as they are married.

At the end of the wedding ceremony joyful music is played. Then the bride and groom walk up the aisle together.

### The Wedding Celebration

When the ceremony is over, the celebration can begin.

First the bride and groom and their attendants and families form a *receiving line*. One by one each wedding guest greets them and gives them their good wishes. The wedding guests may be asked to sign a guest book. Then the bride and groom will have a list to keep of all the people who came to their wedding.

Food and drinks are served as part of most wedding celebrations.

When punch or wine is served, people often make *toasts*. A toast is a shared good wish. The person making the toast holds up his glass. Then he or she says something like, "May the bride and groom live a long and happy life together." Then to show agreement with the toast everyone else lifts up a glass and drinks.

Some wedding celebrations include a meal. Others just serve snacks. However, the highlight of almost every wedding celebration is the cake. Most wedding cakes are like works of art. They often have many layers and all kinds of beautiful decorations. Usually the icing is white. Often the cake is white too. However, in some places it is a custom for wedding cakes to be fruitcake or some other flavor.

One popular tradition is that the bride and groom must cut the first piece of cake together. Then they must feed each other a bite.

At many wedding celebrations there is dancing. Often the bride and groom begin by dancing together. Then everyone else joins them.

When the wedding celebration is over, it is time for the bride and groom to leave on their *honeymoon.* Often a newly married couple take a trip or a vacation right after their wedding. After all the excitement of the wedding, the honeymoon is a chance for them to be alone together.

Just before leaving on her honeymoon a bride often throws her bouquet to all the unmarried girls at the wedding. It is a belief that the girl who catches the bouquet will be the next to marry. Sometimes the groom throws the bride's garter to the unmarried men. In olden times, women wore garters to hold up their stockings. Today, a garter is worn just for fun. Another belief is that if an unmarried girl puts a piece of wedding cake under her pillow, she will dream of her future husband.

## Wedding Customs

Many of the wedding customs we practice today go back to ancient times. Long ago people believed in magic. They thought that certain objects or actions could bring good or bad luck. Today we know that most of these old beliefs are not true. Even so, many of them have become part of wedding traditions.

For instance, it was believed that throwing rice helped a newly married couple to have many children. The custom of a bride carrying fruit or flowers also began because they were supposed to help her have children.

A bride is supposed to have good luck, according to tradition, if she wears something old, something new, something borrowed, and something blue. For intance, she might carry an antique handkerchief, wear a new dress, a piece of borrowed jewelry, and have a blue garter. Another old belief is that it is bad luck for a bride and groom to see each other on their wedding day before the ceremony.

In other parts of the world people have wedding customs that are different from ours.

In some places parents still choose who their children will marry. Sometimes the bride's family must give property or money to the groom before the couple can marry. This is called the bride's *dowry*. Sometimes the groom must pay a "bride price" to the bride's father for his bride. Among certain African tribes this is usually a herd of cattle or other animals.

Usually marriages are only between one man and one woman. However, in some places a man may have more than one wife or a woman may have more than one husband. In most countries, including the United States, it is against the law for anyone to marry more than one person at a time.

### Wedding Anniversaries

Many husbands and wives celebrate the date of their wedding each year. This is their *wedding anniversary*. A husband and wife may give each other presents on their wedding anniversary. They may also celebrate by doing something special such as going out to a restaurant or to the theater.

Sometimes people give a party to celebrate their wedding anniversary. When people have been married for many years, their anniversary is a special celebration. Perhaps you have helped your parents or your grandparents celebrate a wedding anniversary. The twenty-fifth anniversary is called the silver wedding anniversary. The fiftieth anniversary is called the golden wedding anniversary.

Each anniversary year has its own symbol. It is a custom to give anniversary gifts that are made of the symbol for that year.

Here is a list of most anniversary years and their symbols.

| | | | |
|---|---|---|---|
| **1st** | paper | **13th** | lace |
| **2nd** | cotton | **14th** | ivory |
| **3rd** | leather | **15th** | crystal |
| **4th** | linen | **20th** | china |
| **5th** | wood | **25th** | silver |
| **6th** | iron | **30th** | pearl |
| **7th** | wool or copper | **35th** | coral |
| **8th** | bronze | **40th** | ruby |
| **9th** | pottery or china | **45th** | sapphire |
| **10th** | tin or aluminum | **50th** | gold |
| **11th** | steel | **55th** | emerald |
| **12th** | silk | **60th** | diamond |

### Divorce and Remarriage

In most marriage ceremonies people promise to stay married for their whole lives. However, sometimes two people who are married find that they are very unhappy together. They decide that they do not want to be married any more. Then they get a *divorce*.

A divorce is a legal process. Today nearly one third of all marriages end in divorce. A person who is divorced may marry again.

A woman whose husband dies becomes a *widow*. A man whose wife dies becomes a *widower*.

If a divorced or widowed mother remarries, her new husband becomes her children's stepfather. If a divorced

or widowered father remarries, his new wife becomes his children's stepmother. If both the man and woman have children, then their children become stepsisters and stepbrothers. If your mother or father marries someone else and has children, the children are your half-brothers or half-sisters.

Thousands of people get married every day of the year. In the United States June is one of the most popular months for weddings. The weather then is warm and people who have been in school are on vacation.

It is fun to go to a wedding. You may have the chance to go to the wedding of a friend or relative. When you grow up, you may get married one day, too.

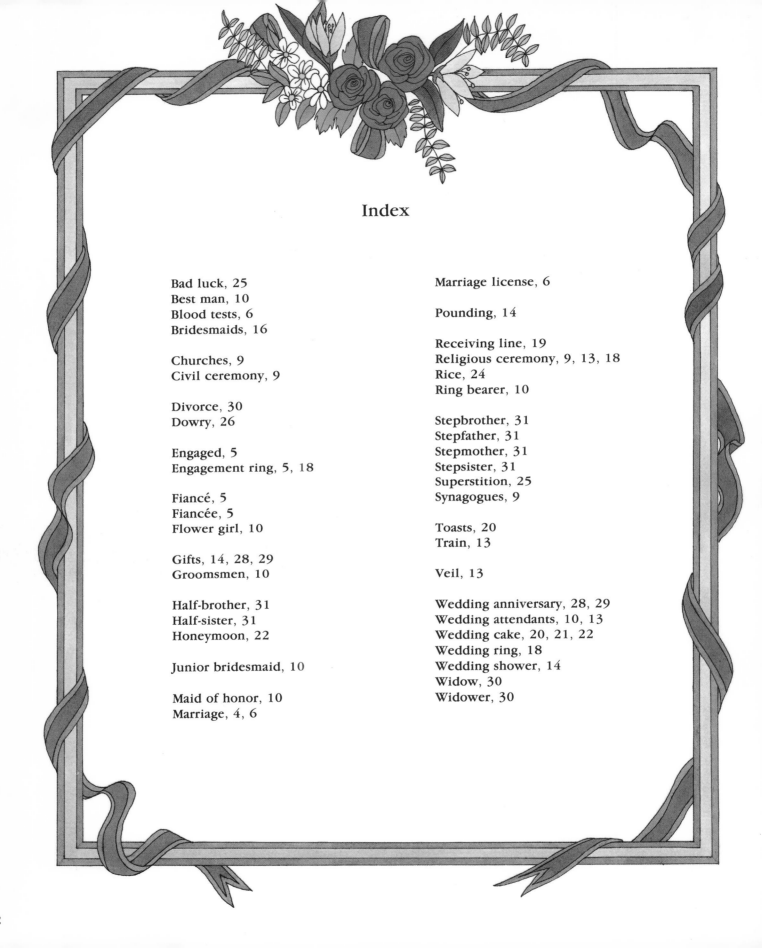

# Index